# How Do Our Eyes See?

## Carol Ballard

HODDER
Wayland

an imprint of Hodder Children's Books

# How Our Bodies Work

How Do Our Eyes See?

How Do Our Ears Hear?

How Do We Taste and Smell?

How Do We Feel and Touch?

How Do We Think?

How Do We Move?

**Editor:** Ruth Raudsepp
**Illustrators:** Kevin Jones Associates and Michael Courtney
**Designer:** Phil Jackson

First published in Great Britain in 1997 by Wayland (Publishers) Ltd
Reprinted in 2001 by Hodder Wayland, an imprint of Hodder Children's Books

© Hodder Wayland 1997

**British Library Cataloguing in Publication Data**
Ballard, Carol
How Do Our Eyes See? – (How Our Bodies Work)
1. Eye –Juvenile literature 2. Vision – Juvenile literature
I. Title II. Jones, K. III Courtney, M.
612.8′4

ISBN 0 7502 3460 1

**Picture Acknowledgements**
The author and publishers thank the following for use of their photographs:
Chapel Studios 4, 5 (top), 7, 22; Chris Fairclough *cover*, 13, 21, 28;
Gary Fry/RNIB 27; Robert Harding 4, 16; Reflections 17; Tony Stone *title page*, 19;
Zefa *contents page*, 5, 18, 20, 23 and 29.
The remaining pictures are from the Wayland Picture Library.

Typeset by Phil Jackson
Printed in Italy by G Canale & C. S.p. A.

# Contents

# Eyes

Our eyes are very important. We use them to find out about the world around us.

Our eyes help to keep us safe. We use them to look for traffic before we cross the road. We also use them to stop us from bumping into things.

▲
Would you enjoy your favourite television programme if you could not see the screen?

▲
◀ We use our eyes to look out for warning signs and signals.

Our eyes allow us to enjoy the world we live in. If we look carefully, we can see tiny animals and plants, beautiful countryside and

wonderful views. In cities there are interesting buildings which we often walk past without even noticing. This book will tell you more about your eyes and how they work.

▲
◄ Our eyes enable us to see to read, write and use a computer.

5

# Look at Your Eyes

When you look at your eyes you can see that they are made up of many parts.

Eyebrows are ridges of skin with short, flat hairs attached. They keep dust and sweat out of the eyes, and protect them against bright sunlight.

▲
A camel's long eyelashes help to protect its eyes from sand and bright sunlight.

Eyelids and eyelashes prevent dust and dirt getting in the eyes. Eyelids keep the eyes moist. When you blink, tear fluid is spread over the surface of your eyes.

◄ Members of a family often have the same colour eyes.

The white part of the eye is called the **sclera**. At the centre of the eye, the sclera is clear so that light can pass through it. This clear part is called the **cornea**.

The coloured part of the eye is called the **iris**. At the centre of each eye is a black circle called the **pupil**. This is a hole which lets light into the eye.

The colour of the iris depends on the amount of **pigment** in it. Brown eyes have a lot of pigment, blue eyes have less.

▼

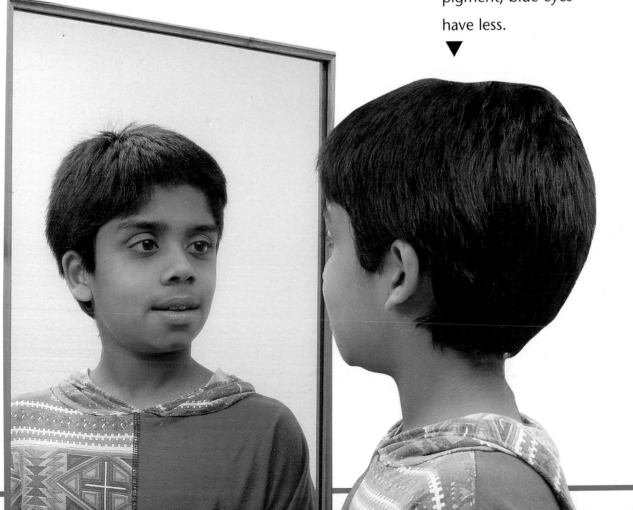

# Inside an Eye

Your eye is like a soft, hollow ball filled with liquid and jelly. Inside the eye, the ball is divided into two parts called chambers. The small front chamber is filled with a watery liquid. The other larger chamber is filled with a soft jelly. The jelly and the liquid make the eyes solid and shaped like a ball.

Between the two chambers is a clear disc called the **lens**. This is held in place by rings of muscles.

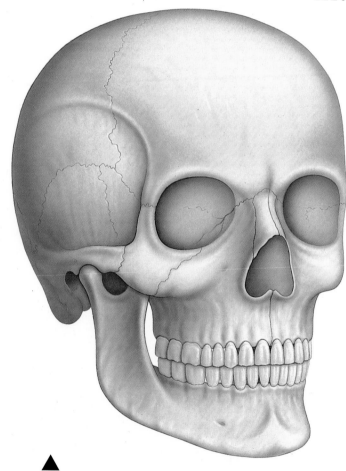

▲

Each eyeball lies inside a bony hollow in the skull. These hollows are strong and protect the eyes from injury.

At the back of the eye is a layer called the **retina**.
The lens bends the light as it enters the eye
to **focus** on the retina. The retina reacts
when light hits it and sends
a message along the
**optic nerve** to
the brain.

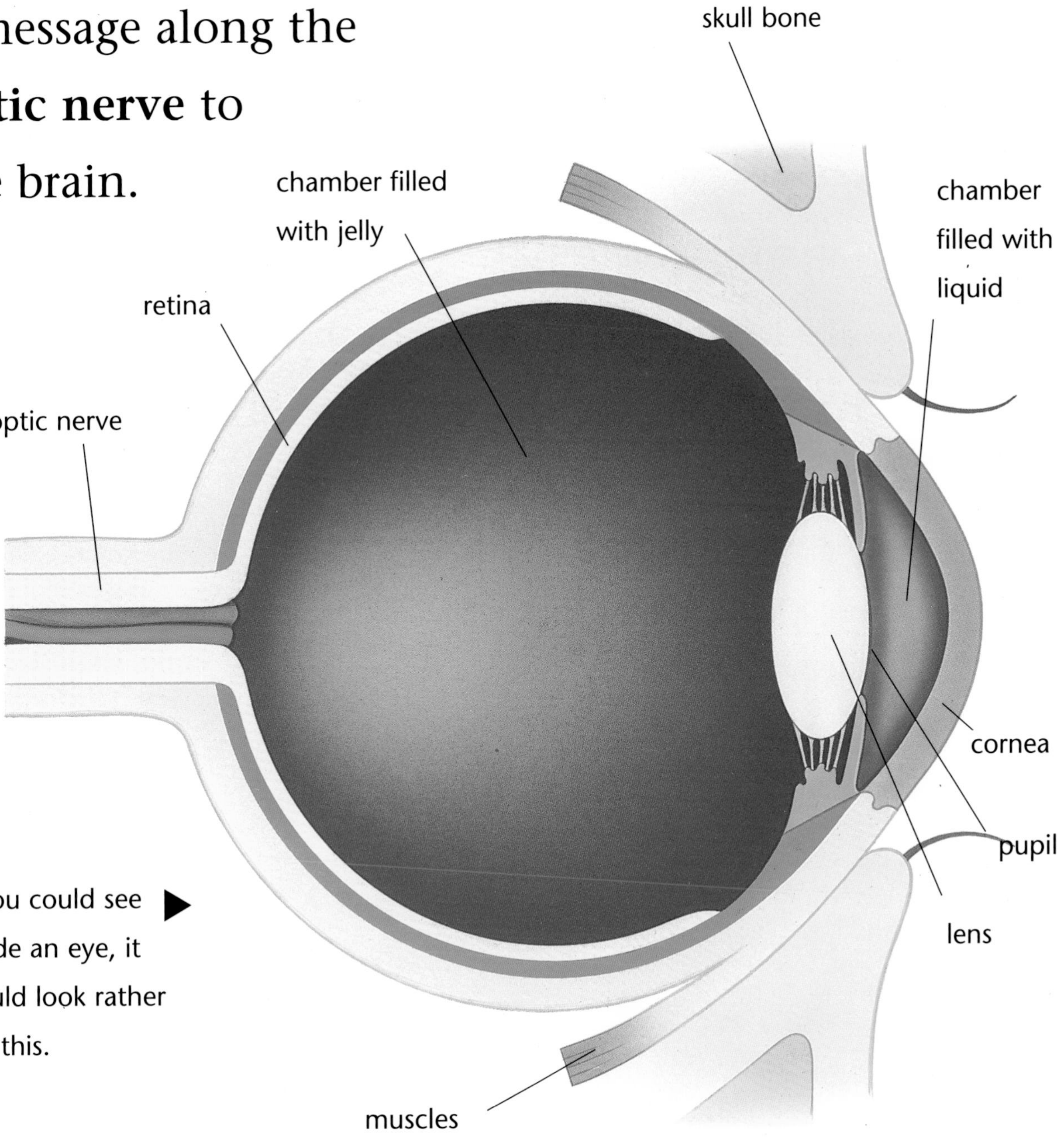

skull bone

chamber filled
with jelly

chamber
filled with
liquid

retina

optic nerve

cornea

pupil

lens

If you could see ▶
inside an eye, it
would look rather
like this.

muscles

# How Do Eyes Work?

We need light to be able to see. Imagine you are looking at a tree. Light from the sun falls on the tree. It bounces off the tree and travels to your eyes. Light passes through the cornea, which bends it a little. It then passes through the front chamber and pupil to the lens. As the light rays pass through the lens, they are bent more. They then pass through the back chamber of your eye to the retina.

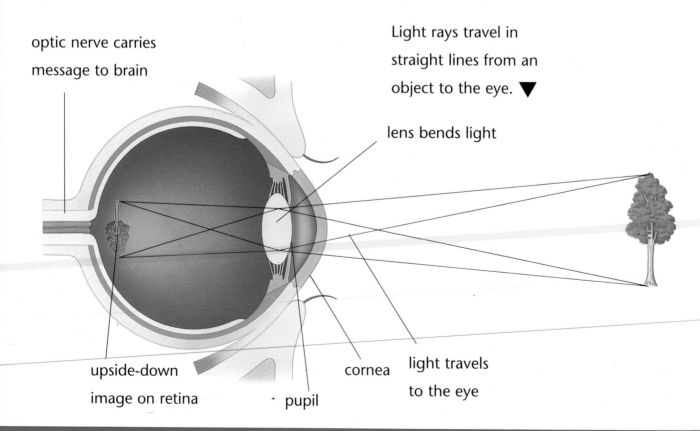

optic nerve carries
message to brain

Light rays travel in
straight lines from an
object to the eye. ▼

lens bends light

upside-down
image on retina

cornea

pupil

light travels
to the eye

When light lands on the retina an **image** of the tree is formed. Because the lens bends the light, the image on the retina is upside-down.

The retinas of both eyes send messages about the tree to the brain. The brain sorts both messages and you 'see' the tree. All this happens so quickly that it seems to take no time at all.

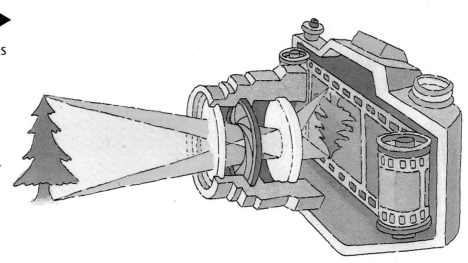

Your eye is like a ▶ camera. Light passes through a hole and is bent by a lens. A picture is formed at the back of the eye. In a camera, the picture is on a film.

# Light and Dark

We can only see clearly if the right amount of light enters our eyes. If the light is too bright, we screw our faces up. This pulls our eyelids closer together and shuts out some of the light.

▲
Cats' eyes have an extra layer inside. This reflects any light that shines on them, so they seem to glow in the dark.

The size of the pupils controls how much light enters the eyes. In bright light, the pupils close until they are just a tiny hole. This keeps out a lot of light. In dim light, the pupils open wide to let in as much light as possible.

◀ Reflective strips on this girl's rucksack will help motorists to see her in the dark.

12

Look carefully at your eyes in a mirror. Can you see how big your pupils are? Now shut your eyes and cover them with your hands. Count slowly to one hundred. Open your eyes and look in the mirror straightaway. How big are your pupils now? Can you explain why they change?

13

▲ Pupils are large in dim light.

▲ We can see clearly in normal light.

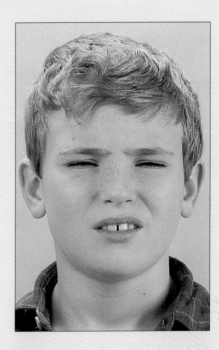

▲ We screw our eyes up in bright light.

# Near, Far and Wide

You can judge distances and shapes because you have two eyes. When you look at something, each eye has a slightly different view of it and sends a different message to your brain. Your brain puts the two messages together and works out a balanced view.

When you look at a cube like this, your left eye sees more of the red side and your right eye sees more of the green side. The brain puts this information together and you get a balanced view. ▼

To see objects at different distances each lens has to change its shape. To see near objects, each lens becomes fatter.

To see distant objects, each lens becomes thinner.

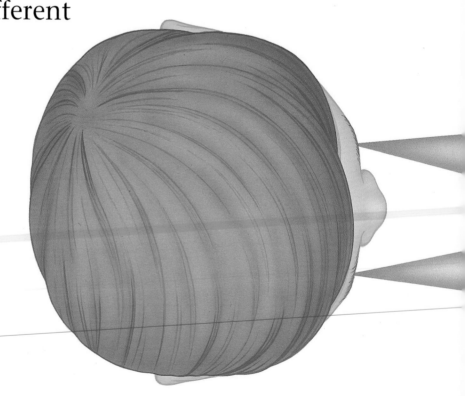

To see things at the
side and behind, we
have to turn our
heads. To find out
how far to the side

you can see, look straight ahead at
something. First, get a friend to stand
behind you and then slowly walk
around you in a circle. Keep staring
straight ahead, and tell your friend
to stop when you can see
him or her.

▲

A hawk's eyes are at the
front of its head so it
can find its prey ahead.
A rabbit's eyes are on
the sides of its head so
it has an all-around view
of any danger.

15

# Seeing in Colour

The retina is made up of millions of **cells**. There are two types of cell in the retina that react to light. These are called rods and cones.

**Eye**

retina

cones respond

light rays

signal sent to brain

**Television**

electron beam

television screen

phosphor dots respond

picture seen by viewer

▲

Each retina is like a living television screen. Electronic receptors in television screens detect red, green or blue light.

Rods **detect** the amount of light that lands on them. Cones detect the colour of the light that lands on them. When you look at a toy, the rods tell the brain how light or dark the toy is. The cones tell the brain what colour the toy is.

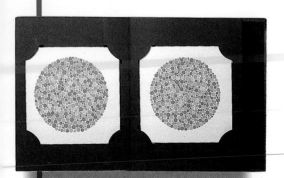

◄ People who are colour-blind may not see the numbers 29 and 57 among the dots.

16

There are three types of cone cell. Each cone cell reacts to just one of the primary colours of light - red, green or blue. If you look at a red apple, the red cone cells react but the blue and green cone cells do not.

People who cannot see a full range of colours are colour-blind. To someone who is red-green colour-blind, a red apple and green grass would look the same colour.

This boy is having ▶ his eyes tested for colour-blindness.

# Do You Need Glasses?

People wear glasses
for different reasons.
Short-sighted people
can see objects that are
close to them, but objects
far away from them are blurred.
Their glasses help them to see
distant objects more clearly.

▲
You should be able to read a
book easily if you hold it about
30cm away from your eyes.

Long-sighted people can see objects that are far
away easily, but find it hard to see
things that are close to
them. Their glasses
help them to see close
objects more clearly.

◄ An optician checks to see that
this child's eyes are healthy.

Some children can see clearly but need to wear glasses to correct other eye problems. Glasses can sometimes help if a child's eyes do not work together, or if they are not developing properly.

Can you read a book and see the computer screen clearly? If not, you may need glasses. Tell an adult so that an eye test can be arranged.

▼

# A Visit to the Optician

Katie is going to the optician's to have her eyes tested. To make sure she gets the right glasses the optician asks her if any of her family wear glasses or have eye problems, and if she is taking any medicines. The optician asks her if she has had any headaches.

▲ Contact lenses are tiny lenses that fit on the front of each eye. They need careful cleaning.

◄ The optician checks that Katie can read the different-sized letters on the chart.

The optician asks Katie to read some letters on a chart. First, she reads with both eyes together. Then the optician covers up each eye in turn and she reads the chart with each eye. He shines a light into Katie's eyes to look inside them and check the retina at the back of each eye.

Once the optician has finished all his tests, he knows which lenses Katie needs to help her see clearly.

An optician takes ▶ measurements to make sure that this girl's glasses will fit properly.

# As You Grow

Babies, when they are first born, cannot see tiny objects or a lot of detail. After a few months, their eyes can follow a moving toy or person. They do not start to see really clearly until they are a couple of years old.

Young children may need glasses to help them see. They cannot read letters, and some are too young to talk, so opticians use cards with patterns and pictures to test their eyesight.

▲
People often need more than one pair of glasses as they get older, but they only wear one at a time!

◄ A baby can see movements and shapes but cannot see details clearly.

Many children start to wear glasses during their first years at school. Some will need to wear them for the rest of their lives. Others will need to wear them for just a few years until the problem is corrected.

As they get older, some people find that they cannot see as well as they did when they were younger. Wearing glasses or contact lenses helps them to see more clearly.

▼

23

# Optical Illusions

Sometimes the brain gets confused about what it sees. These pictures are called optical illusions. Have a look at them. What do you see? Usually, the brain uses information from the eyes and memory to make sense of what you are looking at, but sometimes the brain can get it wrong.

▲
▶

What do you see? Two black faces or one white candlestick? A young girl or an old witch? There are two images in each picture. Your eyes send all the information and your brain has to choose which you see.

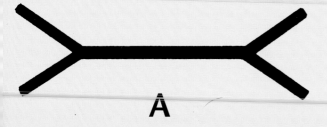

**A**

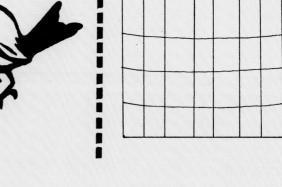

**B**

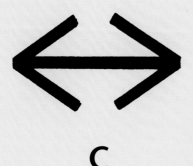

**C**

25

▲

Look carefully at these lines. Which do you think is longest, A, B or C? Now measure them with a ruler. Surprised? The short, outside lines trick your brain. Those on A make the line look longer and those on C make it look shorter.

▲

Put a strip of thin card upright on the dotted line. Look at the bird and the cage. Gradually move your head closer to the page until your nose rests on the card. What happens? Your brain gets a picture of a bird from your left eye and a picture of a cage from your right eye. It has to put the information together so you see the bird inside the cage. (If you don't see the bird inside the cage try a taller or shorter piece of card.)

# Blindness

For **blind** people to lead **independent** lives they need special help.

A guide dog means that a blind person can go outside safely. Guide dogs are trained to guide their owner around obstacles such as lamp posts.

The owner gives the dog instructions by pulling on its special harness.

◀ A guide dog can help a blind person to move around safely.

THE TIME IS THREE MINUTES PAST ELEVEN

▲ There are many objects specially designed to help blind people live a normal life.

Many blind people read using a special alphabet called **braille**. A pattern of raised dots stands for each letter and the person reads it by feeling the dots with their fingers.

Instead of lights and signs, blind people often rely on sound. They can tell the time by using a talking watch. A special clip on the side of a cup bleeps when liquid touches it, so the person knows when the cup is full. Blind people are very neat and tidy. They put things down carefully so they know exactly where things are the next time they want them.

This blind girl is reading a braille ▶ book. The machine in front of her is called a brailler which she uses to type in braille.

# Look After Your Eyes

▲
A balanced diet provides the vitamins you need for healthy eyes.

It is important to look after your eyes, whether or not you wear glasses. Here are some suggestions about how to keep your eyes healthy.

Computer and television screens can be bad for your eyes if you sit in front of them for a long time without a break. When watching the television try not to sit too close. It can be tempting to hold a book right under your nose when you read, but it is much better to hold it about 30 cm away.

▲
You can get goggles made with your lenses so that you can see more easily in the swimming pool.

If you do wear glasses or contact lenses, visit the optician regularly to have your eyes tested. Follow the optician's advice and wear your glasses when you are supposed to. If you play a lot of sport, wearing safety glasses can reduce the risk of an eye injury.

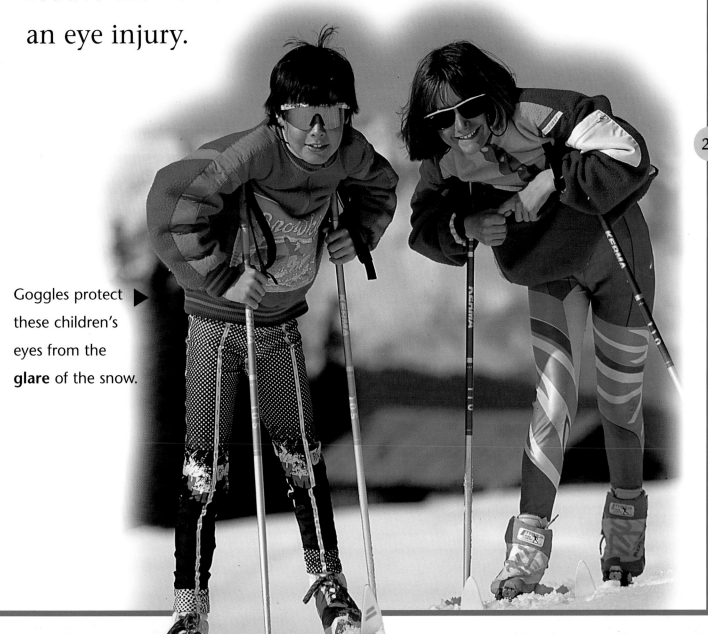

Goggles protect these children's eyes from the **glare** of the snow.

# Glossary

**blind**  Unable to see.

**braille**  An alphabet of raised dots.

**cells**  The millions of tiny building blocks that make up the body.

**cornea**  The clear covering of the front of the eyeball.

**detect**  To notice or pick up information.

**focus**  To produce a clear image.

**glare**  Bright strong sunlight.

**image**  A picture made by light.

**independent**  To be able to look after oneself.

**iris**  The coloured part of the eye.

**lens**  The clear disc which bends light to focus on the retina.

**optic nerve** The nerve which carries messages from the eye to the brain.

**pigment** A substance in the iris which gives it colour.

**pupil** The hole which lets light into the eye.

**retina** The back layer of the eye which is sensitive to light.

**sclera** The thick white covering of most of the eyeball that gives the eye its rounded shape.

# Books to Read

*My Body* (Topic Box series) by Brian Moses (Wayland, 1995).

*My Book of Senses* by Neil Ardley (Dorling Kindersley, 1992).

*The Senses – Seeing* (First Starts series) by Lillian Wright (Watts, 1994).

# Index